SUPER SCIENCE

MATERIALS

WRITTEN BY

Harriet Williamson-Brundle

KidHaven PUBLISHING

Published in 2027 by
KidHaven Publishing, an Imprint of Greenhaven Publishing, LLC
2544 Clinton St., Buffalo, NY 14224

Written by: Harriet Williamson-Brundle
Edited by: Nicola Chave
Designed by: Amelia Harris

Cataloging-in-Publication Data

Names: Harvey, Valerie.
Title: Materials / Valerie Harvey.
Description: Buffalo, NY : KidHaven Publishing, 2027. | Series: Super science | Includes glossary and index.
Identifiers: ISBN 9781534570436 (pbk.) | ISBN 9781534570443 (library bound) | ISBN 9781534570450 (ebook)
Subjects: LCSH: Materials--Juvenile literature. | Materials science--Juvenile literature.
Classification: LCC TA403.2 H378 2027 | DDC 620.11--dc23

Printed in China

CPSIA compliance information: Batch #QS27KH: For further information contact Greenhaven Publishing LLC at 1-844-317-7404.

Please visit our website, www.greenhavenpublishing.com. For a free color catalog of all our high-quality books, call toll free 1-844-317-7404 or fax 1-844-317-7405.

Find us on

Image Credits. All images courtesy of Shutterstock.com, unless otherwise stated.
Cover – Jhon Percy Ticona Mamani, Leremy. Recurring – Dedraw Studio, Leremy. 4–5 – PeopleImages. 6–7 – FAMILY STOCK, NIKS ADS. 8–9 – kasakphoto, conzorb, Daria Nipot, Tatyana Soares. 10–11 – SizeSquares, PLCNSK, Tatiana Diuvbanova, Margarita0192. 12–13 – Sergey Ryzhov, Ratchat, New Africa. 14–15 – Luka C Photography, Lena Ivanova. 16–17 – rai106, ziedaypict, Dipak Shelare, Golden Shrimp, MUHAMMAD ASNAWI 15. 18–19 – Kostikova Natalia, Juice Flair, Sharomka, CREATIVE KNIT DESIGN, sdx15, Gelpi. 20–21 – Jr images, arthierry. 22–23 – Graphic421.

CONTENTS

Words that look like this can be found in the glossary on page 24.

SUPER START!

Science is all about asking questions and trying out ideas to find out how things work. Every question helps us find out something new about our world.

Meet our science superhero, Captain Curious. He is going to help us find out all about materials and their different superhero skills. There might even be some materials you recognize!

WHAT IS A MATERIAL?

Materials are what things are made of. They help build the world around us. Some types of materials we see every day include plastic, metal and glass.

Your clothes, toys and bed are all made of different materials.

Different materials are really good at different jobs and can be used to build different things. Each type of material feels, looks, and acts differently. These are all known as a material's properties.

MIGHTY MATERIALS

Just like superheroes, every material has its own special powers. Some are bendy, some are strong, and others are see-through.

Materials often have more than one superpower.

Not every type of material is able to do every job. It's important to use the right material to match what we need it to do.

MEET THE MATERIALS: WOOD

Wood comes from trees. Some types of wood are light, while others are very heavy and strong. We use wood to make houses, toys, and even the paper for this book!

We can use wood for so many different things.

Wood can be cut, carved, and shaped into what we need it to be. Wood has been used by humans for thousands of years. It's a true super-material!

MEET THE MATERIALS: PLASTIC

Plastic is a <u>human-made</u> material. It can be molded into almost any shape. We use plastic for bottles, toys, shopping bags, and many other everyday things.

Plastic has lots of different properties that make it useful. It can be light, bendy, strong, and waterproof. It can also be smooth, hard, or soft.

MEET THE MATERIALS: GLASS

Glass is a hard, human-made material. Glass is transparent, which means it is see-through. Glass is used for windows, bottles, jars, and glasses.

Glass is made by heating sand until it melts and then shaping it. When it cools down again, it is a solid piece of glass. That's an amazing superpower to have!

MEET THE MATERIALS: METAL

Metal is a strong material found deep underground in rocks. Metal is heated and shaped to make lots of everyday items, such as cars, cans, and pots and pans.

Metal has lots of amazing properties, so we use it to make many different things!

There are lots of different types of metal and they each have their own superpowers.

ALUMINUM: LIGHT
PERFECT FOR CANS

IRON: STRENGTH
GREAT FOR MAKING BRIDGES

GOLD: SUPER SHINE
MAKES BEAUTIFUL JEWELRY

TITANIUM:
STRONG AND LIGHT
JUST RIGHT FOR
BICYCLES

MEET THE MATERIALS: CLOTH

Cloth is a soft material that is used to make clothes, curtains, blankets, and lots of other everyday things. Cloth is made from fibers. Some fibers come from nature, like wool. Others are human-made.

Cloth is flexible, too.

The different fibers that cloth is made from can affect its properties.

COTTON IS SOFT AND COMFORTABLE.

WOOL KEEPS US VERY WARM.

SILK IS SMOOTH AND SHINY.

DENIM IS THICK AND TOUGH.

MATERIAL SUPERPOWERS!

Each of the materials we have met so far have the perfect superpowers for what they are used for. But when we're looking for a material to do a job, how do we choose the right one?

Before choosing a material, ask yourself questions like:

- What do I want the object to do?
- Does it need to be strong?
- Does it need to keep things dry?
- Does it need to be see-through?

SUPER SCIENCE CHALLENGE

Are you ready to become a science superhero? Take this quiz and check your answers on page 23.

1. Wood comes from trees. (True/False)
2. Plastic is always soft. (True/False)
3. Metals can be strong and heavy. (True/False)
4. Glass can be easily broken. (True/False)
5. All materials have the same properties. (True/False)

You have completed this Super Science book and have now become a

★ SCIENCE SUPERHERO! ★

Keep exploring, asking questions, and discovering amazing things about the world.

Answers:
1. True. 2. False: Plastic can be hard or soft. 3. True. 4. True. 5. False: Each material has its own properties that make it different from others.

GLOSSARY

CARVED	cut or shaped
FIBERS	things that are like threads
FLEXIBLE	having the ability to bend and stretch
HUMAN-MADE	created by humans and not natural
SOLID	firm and stable; not a liquid
WATERPROOF	stops water from getting through

INDEX